Christmas at the Mission

A Cat's View of Catholic Customs and Beliefs

Sula, Parish Cat at Old Mission

Copyright 2017 by MSI Press LLC

All rights reserved. No part of this book may be reproduced or utilized in any form or by any means, electronic or mechanical, including photocopying, recording, or by any information storage and retrieval system, without permission in writing from the publisher.

For information, contact

MSI Press, LLC
1760 Airline Hwy, #203
Hollister, CA 95023

Sula's voice: Betty Lou Leaver

Cover design and book layout: Carl Leaver

Front cover photo by Betty Lou Leaver

Back cover collage photographs, clockwise from left by Rick Edge, Jewell Gentry, Betty Lou Leaver, and Kaleen Scargill

Illustrations by Zhenya Yanovich

Copyeditor: Geri Hendeson

Proofreading assistance provided by Van Wolverton

Source of Sula's biographical information: Mary Anzar

Library of Congress Control Number: 2017945387

ISBN: 978-1-942891-39-0

Contents

About Me and This Book 3

12 Days of Christmas 9

Advent 15

Angels 21

Bells 25

Candles 29

Christmas Carols 35

Christmas Mass 41

Christmas Tree 47

Creche 53

Decorations 57

Epiphany 63

Gifts 69

Jesse Tree 73

Mary 77

Mary Candle 81

Prayer 85

Shepherds 91

St. Lucy Cakes 95

St. Nicholas 101

Wreaths 107

**References and Sources
for More Information** 111

Sula, Parish Cat, San Juan Bautista Mission

Sula, Parish Cat, San Juan Bautista Mission

O holy night, the starts are brightly shining...

About Me and This Book

I love Christmas! Who doesn't? Everyone I know loves Christmas, but then they are all people. I am a cat, but I enjoy celebrating Christmas with my people friends and with my Boss. Christmas is a special time for my Boss. He is the One and Only, you know, the One who brought His plan to life that first Christmas—except no one knew then it was Christmas.

As for me, if you have read either of my other books (if not, please do), you know as much about me as it is possible to know. For those who have not read them yet, I can tell you my tale in a nutshell. It is pretty simple, partly because the beginning is rather cloudy, and I only know what the people at the Mission Gift Shop remember about me some 12 years ago. Yes, I am getting to be quite a big girl now with my own set of life experiences. It seems that I was always in San Juan Bautista, a beautiful Mission town in the Mexican tradition. Lots of Spanish spoken here, so I have had to learn to meow and respond in two languages. People say that they saw me at the cemetery (not much action there) and later at City Hall (a little more action there, but still rather boring and not appealing to me). Then, I heard the bells pealing at the Mission across from City Hall and I trotted over to see what was going on. Though still a kitten, I knew I had found my mission in life: to minister to those at the Mission with the help of God, (my Boss,) and St. Francis. I became a "Catolic" immediately. The rest of the story—how I minister, how I survived two bouts of cancer, how I lost my ears, and how I made so many life-long friends at the Mission—is told in my first two books, *Surviving Cancer, Healing People: One Cat's Story* and *Tale of a Mission Cat*.

The purpose of this book is not to be an exhaustive catalogue of information about all aspects of Christmas or even about Catholic dogma about Christmas. For those who were hoping that I had put together such a catalogue, I apologize for any disappointment and have included for your reading delight a list of references at the end of this book that will take you to more authoritative and more exhaustive sources. The purpose of this book is to share the joy of my Christmas with you—what Christmas means to me as a Catholic cat—in pictures along with some descriptions of Catholic traditions seen in those pictures.

Where I am aware of the origins of various customs, I mention them. Some do not come from where you think. Some, like feasting, having fun, giving gifts, and taking a rest from work, have parallels in pagan traditions—and that is okay. If whatever we do, we do for the glory of God, other parallels are merely parallels, nothing of significance but perhaps something of interest.

I also include some suggested songs related to each custom. You will have to Google the whole song. Because most songs are copyrighted, I cannot include all the words—and all the words would take too much space, anyway. So, if you like the first line of the song, put it into your browser and find the rest of the song and the music that goes with it. It will be your special Christmas treasure hunt! Some of these songs are truly treasures!

Oh, and one thing I do not include in this book because it is a year-round sacrament, not a Christmas tradition, is confession. That said, watching people who come to confession, I can tell that the Sacrament of Reconciliation is very important to them and brings them peace. During Advent, most churches offer large-scale confession opportunities. If anyone is willing to take advice from a cat, I say "go for it; don't pass up any opportunity for reconciliation." Every week I see the wonderful effect it has on the few people who show up.

I do want to thank the elves who helped me prepare this book. Possibly the most important elf is Zhenya Yanovich, who drew all the pictures of me. Zhenya lives in Moscow, Russia, but when he is drawing me, it seems like he is right next door.

The photography elves (back cover, clockwise) were Rick Edge, Jewell Gentry, Stacey Gentry, Betty Lou Leaver, and Kaleen Scargill. Let me tell you about the pictures they took here since I have no other place to talk about them. The picture at the top left is me sleeping in the nativity scene, taken by Rick Edge. In the upper right photograph, taken by Jewell Gentry, I am listening to the hymns at our Mission on Christmas Eve. In the lower left photograph, take by Kaleen Scargill, I am resting in the blessed rays of the sun drifting into the Mission through its upper windows during the Winter Solstice, and in the lower right, I am sleeping at the feet of Our Lady in the Mission chapel, a most comforting place to rest. My bio picture is a special gift of Stacey Gentry, my official photographer.

Sula, Parish Cat, San Juan Bautista Mission

Sula, Parish Cat, San Juan Bautista Mission

On the first day of Christmas, my true love sent to me a partridge in a pear tree...

12 Days of Christmas

The twelve days of Christmas refer to the period extending from Christmas to Epiphany. The song you just read and maybe even sang in your head is well known both to Catholics and to those not in the Church. It is a secular tribute to something sacred, but many people do not know the sacred part.

Do you know that there are three feasts during the 12 days of Christmas? They date from the fifth century and all focus on the incarnation of the Word of God (Christ) as the baby Jesus, human like us—well, like you; I am a cat. The three feasts are the Feast of St. Stephen, the Feast of St. John the Evangelist, and the Feast of the Holy Innocents.

The Feast of St. Stephen is first—on December 26. St. Stephen was one of the disciples. He was known for helping the poor. For that reason, we Catholics often give leftovers to the poor on December 26. (Giving them new stuff is pretty okay, too.) St. Stephen was also one of the first deacons. Did you know that we have had deacons for 20 centuries? Like all of Jesus's disciples except John the Evangelist, St. Stephen was martyred; in fact, he was the first to be martyred. People who did not like Jesus put St. Stephen in a hole in the ground, covered him with dirt, and threw stones at him until he died. How painful! That means he died for his faith, like many people have over many centuries and like many people today in some parts of the world still do. Even though dying for one's faith and being able to do that is something very special, I admit that I am very grateful that we Catholics can practice our faith in peace here in beautiful San Juan Bautista, which is sunny even at Christmas time, and not have to worry about people throwing stones at us, nailing us to trees, or even shooting us with guns. We live in a valley clearly blessed by God, and that blessing becomes even more meaningful during the 12 days of Christmas.

The Feast of S. John the Evangelist is next—on December 27. St. John was the only disciple not to be martyred, or so I am told. (I mean, I wasn't there, after all, so I have to take some information as fact based on oral history, people telling people telling other people and, of course, stories written down, which are even better because the details do not change the way they do in oral histories.) John's charism (gift from God) was the ability to write in ways that others understood. He was the one who told us about the Incarnation, writing that the Word became flesh and lived among people, i.e. us, well, you.

The third feast is the Feast of the Holy Innocents—on December 28. Remember how Herod told his soldiers to kill all baby boys under two years of age because he wanted to make sure he wiped out Jesus, who he feared was the Messiah. He was right about that last part; Jesus *was* the Messiah, but he was wrong about the first part. It is always wrong to kill, and these little baby boys were innocent of any wrongdoing. That is why we call them the Holy Innocents. They were the very first to die for Jesus.

One interesting thing that is not often talked about is that during these 12 days, around the first of January, is the time when the baby Jesus was circumcised. It seems like a very important thing, so maybe people ought to talk about it more. If God, in all His great power, became like a baby and submitted Himself to the Jewish law that required babies to be circumcised, what does that tell us today about obedience to the law of God? Many consider Jesus to be a great revolutionary because He totally changed much of what we think and do when it comes to our relationship to God, yet He was no rebel. He followed the traditions, customs, and laws of Judaism, just like the people of my parish follow the traditions, customs, and laws of Catholicism today. The message of Christ, though, strayed far from traditional thinking. Just think about it: God became a baby; Jesus taught us that the poor and lowly, not the rich, are the first in His kingdom, that political importance does not matter but love of God does. Our Catholic traditions look a lot different from run-of-the-mill human traditions, don't they? I like that! It makes me, a lowly cat, feel very important. I thank God every morning, when I talk to St. Francis in the Mission garden, for considering me special enough to allow me the task of ministering to His people in our parish. That is a Christmas gift that lasts all year.

The 12 days of Christmas end on the epiphany. That is when the Wise Men (or Magi) bring the gifts to baby Jesus, but I will tell you about that later in this book.

Sula, Parish Cat, San Juan Bautista Mission

Sula, Parish Cat, San Juan Bautista Mission

O come, o come, Emmanuel and ransom captive Israel...
(unknown author)

Advent

Advent means that something is coming. What is coming, of course, is the birth of the Christ child. Advent begins 4 Sundays before Christmas and lasts until Christmas eve. Depending upon the year, the First Sunday of Advent can be anywhere between November 27 and December 3.

Advent at Old Mission is beautiful. The church is decorated; people are happy; the priest talks about the coming birth of the Messiah. I like Advent because it is such a happy time. Even people who have problems and are sometimes (or often) gloomy cheer up at Advent.

Not all people are happy, though. I see some from walking the grounds. They don't have homes, and it is hard for them to celebrate. They don't have money for gifts. Our Mission collects money and food for people during Advent and gives it to them right before Christmas. Some of those people attend our Mission; some are in our community; all are friends. Christmas helps us remember God's love for all people because Jesus was sent to be a Messiah for everyone whether or not they went to the right church or worshipped God in prescribed ways, for the righteous and for the sinners. That is reassuring to me because sometimes I do sin—like drinking the Holy Water before Mass or thinking about helping myself to the wafers before they are converted to the Host. After all, I am a common cat, just like the human beings around me are common people—and we all make mistakes and do things we regret.

Advent is a great time to think about those things and take time for confession. Our Mission offers a special time, in addition to the regular times, for confession during Advent.

People keep track of Advent in various ways. One way is with candles, and another way is with calendars.

Advent candles at home are burned down a little each day until Advent is over. At Mass, during Advent, one candle is lit each Sunday for the first four Sundays of Advent.

Advent calendars, first used by Lutherans in the early 19th century, mark the days of Advent. Advent calendars can be made of wood, cardboard, or occasionally, fabric. They can be shaped like rectangles, houses, Christmas trees, or just about any Christmas image. Nowadays, computer geeks (and anyone else) can download or interact online with virtual Advent calendars and even audio Advent calendars. Some are even international, and people from many countries get to share the excitement of Advent. Similarly, in the Nordic countries (Denmark, Finland, Iceland, Norway, and Sweden) there is a radio or television show, *Julekalendar* (Yule calendar, which is another name for a Christmas calendar—in actuality, an audiovisual form of an Advent calendar), which has been airing since 1957. The television and radio stations aim some of these shows for children and others for adults.

Advent calendars have 24 doors, windows, or pockets. Each day another door is opened to find a picture behind it—the Lutherans in the 19th century put Holy Bible verses behind the doors. Today, families often use the opening of a door to say a prayer or share something spiritual with each other. Sometimes a treat, or a other surprise is picked out of a pocket of a fabric Advent calendar. (Hint for my Mission Gift Shop caretakers: I think a cat treat in each pocket would be just purr-fect.) On December 24th, when the days of Advent have been completed and all the doors opened, Christmas has arrived. How exciting to count down in this way—and every day to reflect upon the meaning of Christmas and how wonderful God was to send us such a permanent gift.

Christmas at the Mission

Other Advent decorations include Advent wreaths. The wreath holds echoes of Easter as it reminds us of Christ's victory over death. The wreath holds four candles an equal distance apart. I like wreaths…I like peeking through them!

Finally, Advent is known for the great antiphon O's. What are these? You probably will recognize them once I tell you. On each of the last seven days of Advent, the antiphon prayers summarize the meaning and scope of Advent.

- December 17. O Wisdom, that proceedest from the mouth of the Most High, Reaching from end to end mightily, and sweetly disposing all things: come and teach us the way of prudence.

- December 18. O Lord and Ruler of the house of Israel, Who didst appear unto Moses in the burning bush, and gavest him the law on Sinai: come and redeem us by Thy outstretched arm.

- December 19. O Root of Jesse, Who standest as the Ensign of the people, before Whom kings shall not open their lips; to Whom the Gentiles shall pray: come and deliver us, tarry now no more.

- December 20. O Key of David, and Sceptre of the house of Israel; Who openest, and no man shutteth, Who shuttest, and no man openeth: come and lead the captive from the prison house, and him that sitteth in darkness and the shadow of death.

Sula, Parish Cat, San Juan Bautista Mission

- December 21. O Dawn of the East, Splendor of the eternal Light, and Sun of justice: Come and enlighten them that sit in darkness, and the shadow of death.

- December 22. O King of the gentiles, yea, and the desire thereof, the Cornerstone that makest both one: come and save man, whom Thou hast made out of the slime of the earth.

- December 23. O Emmanuel, our King and Lawgiver, the expectation of all nations and their Salvation: come and save us, O Lord our God.

Now, which of these traditions will you follow this Advent season? There are so many to choose from! If you need help from a cat, come to the Mission and look for me. I will almost always be in one of the pews during any of the Masses.

Sula, Parish Cat, San Juan Bautista Mission

Angels we have heard on high...

Angels

In the Holy Bible, Luke tells us about the important role that the angels played in the birth of Jesus. They were the voices and choir letting the shepherds know the good news.

Angels are messengers from God. In fact, that is what the word, angel, means messenger.

Jesus's birth is not the only time that the angels been involved in the affairs of people. Think about some other times:

- Three angels appeared to Abraham; he gave them food and rest, and they told him that his wife Sarah, who was very, very old, would have a child—and she did: Isaac.

- Jacob wrestled with an angel.

- It was two angels who saved Lot from the destruction of Sodom and Gomorrah.

- An angel appeared to Joshua before the fight for Jericho—and we know that Joshua and his people won, with the help of God.

- An angel rescued Daniel from the lion's den.

- An angel announced to Zacharias that he would have a son, St. John the Baptist.

- It was an angel who convinced Joseph in a dream to marry Mary.

- An angel ministered to Jesus after His temptation in the desert and in the Garden of Gethsemane before His crucifixion, and after He was buried and risen, an angel stood at the entrance to His tomb.

A very important angel, of course, is Gabriel, one of only four angels whose names have been shared in the Holy Bible. Gabriel played a very important role related to the birth of Jesus. He appeared to Mary with the message that God wanted her to bear the Messiah.

The night of Jesus's birth, there was not one angel, or two angels, like at other times. There was a whole host of angels, who came from the heavens to herald the arrival of the Messiah and then returned to the heavens in sight of the shepherds.

Angels played a really important role that night. That is why many Christmas ornaments are forms of angels, including the common topping of the Christmas tree.

It seems that angels do not appear to the world's leaders (not typically), but to the simple folk, like Mary, people who are open to being used by God, and like the shepherds whom the angels knew would spread God's important good news.

Angels play an important role in the lives of many people today. Do you know of anyone today who has had an experience with an angel? I bet you do! Maybe you have yourself. If not, ask around...angels are here and not just on Christmas Day.

Sula, Parish Cat, San Juan Bautista Mission

*I heard the bells on Christmas Day
their old, familiar carols play...*

Bells

The bells pealing at the Mission attracted me to my calling. I love the sound of bells. They usually, though not always, send out a message of joy that reverberates into one's very bones, making me want to do a little hop.

At Christmas, bells are everywhere. Think of all the bells associated with the Christmas season.

Perhaps the very first bells during Advent are those that appear in the hands of the Salvation Army donation collectors. They ring tirelessly to collect money to help those who cannot afford to celebrate Christmas, which is a season that everyone should definitely have a chance to celebrate. I am happy to know that members of our parish help out in this way and many other ways, including collecting our own donations to help.

Bells as decorations abound at Christmas. You can find little ones on Christmas trees, gifts, and wreaths. Images of bells adorn wrapping paper and greeting cards. Bigger bells dangle from doorways in houses, along with holly, ivy, and mistletoe, taking their place alongside trees, nativity scenes, strings of lights and icicles, and charming figurines.

Bells have signaled the arrival of Christmas for a very long time and in different ways, depending upon where you live. In England, the largest bell in the church rings four times the hour before midnight and then all the bells ring at midnight. We don't do that at our Mission. Every country has its own tradition, of course, but I really like that British custom.

Some Catholic churches (also Anglican and Lutheran churches) in other parts of the world ring bells three times a day on Christmas: in the morning, noon, and evening. They are calling Christians to recite the *Lord's Prayer* in honor of the birth of Jesus as the incarnation of God. We don't do that at our Mission, but I am including that information because some readers may live in places where this happens—and because I personally think it is a very nice tradition. Of course, no one really needs a bell to remember to recite the Lord' Payer, or any prayer. My patron saint, St. Francis, urged all of us to pray unceasingly and, if necessary, to use words. I do that. It helps me stay true to my Mission. I need to know what the Boss wants so that I can be obedient. Being obedient is what brings me joy and what brings joy to the people to whom I offer healing at the Boss's encouragement.

Of course, bells are not just part of Christmas. They are everywhere, as part of our lives. Big ones ring before Mass; little ones ring during Mass.

We have a famous belfry at our Mission. You may already know a little about it because our belfry figured prominently in Alfred Hitchcock's movie, *Vertigo*. I won't go into the details because they are pretty somber, but if you have not seen the movie, perhaps you will watch it; you would learn a lot about our Mission and see some pictures taken in 1957 that look almost exactly like the Mission looks today—except for the belfry. Unfortunately, our old belfry fell down in the 1954 earthquake. Alfred Hitchcock really needed our belfry in his movie, so he had one made because our new belfry, which was built a few years later, was not yet finished. Today, you can see Alfred Hitchcock's belfry at the rest stop along Highway 101 that used to be the entrance to our town of San Juan Bautista.

No matter what the belfry looks like, I like the bells. They say to me, "Come! Great things are happening, and you are welcome to participate in them!" Like in my calling...

Sula, Parish Cat, San Juan Bautista Mission

*There's a road that I remember leading to a special place...
It don't take a lot of money to know what riches are: just a
candle in the window and Christmas in your heart.*

Candles

Candles, in Christian tradition, symbolize new light in darkness. It is the light that Jesus brought into a dark world, and it is the light that Jesus brings us today no matter how dark the night or troubled the times.

When I ask people where candles come from and why they are connected with Christmas, they tell me many different things. So, I guess no one really knows. Some of the explanations, though, make some sense, at least to this cat. These explanations, for example:

- Candles were adopted from ancient Winter Solstice celebrations, where they served to remind people that spring was coming—and other Christmas customs seem to have evolved from Winter Solstice celebrations.

- In the Middle Ages, Christians used a large candle to represent the star of Bethlehem.

- Christians call Jesus the "Light of the World;" perhaps this led to the use of Advent candles.

- Jews use candles for Hanukkah (the Festival of Lights, which honors the re-dedication of the Second Temple in Jerusalem two centuries before the birth of Jesus), which usually occurs sometime around Christmas (though Jews use a lunar calendar so sometimes the dates are closer together and sometimes farther apart)—and Christianity has a Jewish foundation though some folks might like to tell me to "scat!" when I say that.

- In earlier days, the only way to light a Christmas tree was with candles; fortunately, we have safer ways today! Can you imagine if one of my curious cousins were to knock over a candle-lit Christmas tree while just wanting to nestle in the fragrant fir branches!

Candles have long been used as decorations. The very first Christmas trees were decorated with candles. Often, people think that the concept of the candle and its message of God sending light to the earth started with the original Christians, but it did not. It started long before then, in a very different way. Pagan ceremonies in ancient times included lighting candles during festivals associated with the Winter solstice, which coincides with Christmas. (One of the pictures on the back cover of this shows me, mellowing in the fading light of the early morning Solstice sunrise at our Mission.) The pagans, of course, used the candles (and bonfires) in a very different way: to beg the sun to return and warm away the cold winter.

Really, it was only after the 18th century, when Christians adopted some of the pagan holiday traditions, that candle-lighting became part of Catholic (and Protestant) Christmas celebrations. In our tradition, they represent the eternal light of Jesus's spirit, which every Christmas helps us to remember. We should remember that every day. Our own solstices may not necessarily occur in December, concurrently with the naturally occurring Winter Solstice. Our darkest personal days could even be at the height of the naturally bright summer. We need Jesus's light as much in our emotionally wintry days as we do in the real winter.

Candles come in different colors. The colors mean different things. For example, white candles remind us of the purity of Christ, and a pink candle represents joy. As Mass, we light one candle each week of the four weeks of Advent. The three purple candles symbolize prayer and preparation, as in getting ready for Jesus to come. They also mean hope, peace, and love, the emotions we associate with the coming of Jesus. The fourth candle, the pink candle, which means joy, is lit on the third Sunday of Advent, which is known as Gaudete (Joy) Sunday. (The priest wears a pink chasuble (robe) that Sunday.

Advent candles used at home have marks that show how many days remain until Christmas. Each day, the candle is lit and allowed to burn down to the next mark, then put out, waiting for the next day to come.

Other important candles are the Mary candle and the Christ candle. Both candles are big and white; in fact, the Mary candle is the Christ candle with a blue ribbon. The Christ candle is a symbol for Christ (duh!) and is lit on Christmas Eve to show that the "Light of the World" has arrived. Some families have the nice habit of keeping the Christ calendar on their table all year round and, following Christmas, light it at every Sunday dinner, reminding them of waiting for Christ, of His coming, and of His resurrection.

Candles are also used in house decorations. Some people put them in their windows, as if telling Mary and Joseph that there *is* room at their home.

Nowadays, though, many people prefer to use the artificial candles—the kind that my cousins cannot knock over and start a house fire! Many dangerous fires in the past led to abandoning taping fire to tree branches!

Sula, Parish Cat, San Juan Bautista Mission

Here we come a-caroling among the leaves so green...

Christmas Carols

Music is such an important part of our life at the Mission. At every Mass we sing hymns, liturgical songs, and excerpts from the *Psalms*. Christmas, though, has special songs. People call them *Christmas carols*.

There are many different Christmas carols. Each carol tells a different part of the story of what happened at and shortly after the birth of Jesus. Here are some. I am sure you know others:

- *O, Little Town of Bethlehem* is about the city where Jesus was born.

- *Silent Night* is about the time when Jesus was born.

- *Away in a Manger* talks about the place where Jesus was born.

- *What Child Is This?* is about Jesus himself.

- *The First Noel* is about the angels telling the shepherds about the birth of Jesus.

- *We Three Kings* is about the magi who brought gifts to the baby Jesus.

Sula, Parish Cat, San Juan Bautista Mission

When people go from house to house in town, singing carols for anyone who will open their doors, it is called caroling. People who moved here from places where there is snow tell me stories about how they used to go caroling in the cold, dark evenings, and when they were done, they gathered at one of the houses for hot cocoa. (Well, not exactly good for a cat; better to give us warm water.)

There is another word for caroling, *wassailing*. It is British. I mention it because one hears that word in some Christmas songs, like *Here We Come A-Wassailing*. (If you don't know that song, just Google it!) Actually, wassailing, which tooK place in England, was a little different from caroling. People who went from door to door, singing carols, carried a bowl of hot punch (the wassail bowl) and offered drinks in exchange for gifts. Interesting how different countries do similar things differently, isn't it?

Years ago, there was a lot more caroling taking place than nowadays. At least, though, some people still do it—and at our Mission, before Midnight Mass, everyone sings carols.

Here is a fun fact about caroling. In old England, when Queen Victoria was the ruler, people would take hand bells (yes, more bells!!) with them. As they sang, they would also play the music on the hand bells. How delightful! Maybe someday people here will do that!

Most of the parishes in our area have a Spanish Mass. For the most part, the customs are the same among the parishioners who attend the Spanish Mass and those who attend the English Mass. However, the Mexicans and Mexican-Americans in our community have a very special tradition, call *Las Posadas*, which look a little like caroling, because they go from house to house in a procession. But there is a big difference in intent and activities. This procession reenacts the life of Joseph and Mary as they are looking for an inn. The children dress up as Mary and Joseph and carry the baby Jesus. Some children are also angels or shepherds. Some carry sticks with bells, like the shepherds'

Christmas at the Mission

rods. To make them, typically they paint broomsticks and sometimes add tinsel. The people in the procession carry candles and sing songs special *Posada* songs as they walk along. At each house they stop it, they are refused entry just like Mary and Joseph were refused. Finally, they reach a house that lets them in—the "crash pad"—like the manger where Joseph and Mary ended up. (Secret! They plan the house in advance.) At that house, they sing. Then they pray *el rosario* (the rosary). Then—they have a feast, with hot chocolate! Think about it. It is cold in December. Everyone needs hot chocolate to warm up. The children look forward to this last house because they get treats in a brown bag: *cacahuates* (peanuts), *los tomys* (hard milk candies), *los galletos* (cookies), and an orange. The treats might be a little different in other parts of the United States and Mexico, but here in our area, these are the expected treats. If the family can afford it, the children get to break a piñata. Everyone takes off their costumes and leaves them at this house when they leave. Why? Because the next day, they will come to this house and get dressed up again—and start another procession that ends at another house. *Las Posadas* last an entire week.

Alas, I do not get to participate in any of these lovely activities. I very cautiously stay around the Mission grounds. I know I can get lost if I stray far—and my Mission is not "out there." It is "in here," That is what is important to me. It is what I love to do, at Christmas or any other time of year.

Sula, Parish Cat, San Juan Bautista Mission

Sula, Parish Cat, San Juan Bautista Mission

Silent night, holy night...

Christmas Mass

I attend all the Christmas Masses. Each is different, and each is important. Of course, every Mass is important because it provides time away from a busy day to worship my Boss and think about the most important things in life.

Christmas Eve Masses come first, and our parish celebrates a couple of kinds of those. In the afternoon of December 24, children and their parents attend an afternoon family Mass. At this Mass, the children reenact the Christmas story. The family Mass is such fun! Children, being unpredictable, do unpredictable things. One year, Mary dropped the baby Jesus doll. A talking doll, it cried out "Mama, Mama!" People tried to stay serious, but some could not stop themselves from laughing. I scampered up into a pew—just in case something else went wrong. Another year three brothers played the three kings—and got into a fight. Boy, did they embarrass their parents, who had just finished telling other people that their boys were their pride and joy. Well, children will be children, but mostly, though, the family Mass is quiet, well enacted, and exciting. Exciting, because the story of Jesus is exciting. Wouldn't you agree?

Midnight Mass comes later, at 11:00, and is usually for the adults although, of course, anyone can go to any Mass, even a cat. The Midnight Mass used to be at midnight and meant to be the first Mass of Christmas Day; it still is in many places. In those cases, often there is another Mass: the Christmas Vigil Mass in the evening. A "vigil" is a time of waiting and preparation, so the Christmas Vigil Mass is meant to prepare for the feast of Christmas. Our Mission sort of combines the two, as probably most American Catholic churches do. So, we have one Mass in the evening. It starts at 10:30 with Christmas carols. I always come early to listen to those, as you can probably tell by looking at the back cover of this book.

The evening of the 24th, no matter how late, has a liturgy associated with getting prepared for Christmas. This is the last day of Advent, and everyone is waiting in joyous expectation for the arrival of the Messiah. The readings reflect great confidence that the Savior is coming.

When the Mass is over, people go home in the cold and dark to wait the dawn and warmth of the new day, the day when they will celebrate the joy of the birth of Jesus. As for me, well, I have a couple of choices. I can sleep overnight on one of the pews or by the altar not far from the tabernacle holding the Body that comforts me. Or, I can sleep outside the gift shop in a cat igloo that one of the parishioners, noticing that I, like the Baby, did not really have a bed, brought me one. How sweet! We have truly generous and kind parishioners at Old Mission San Juan Bautista; they spoil me.

On Christmas Day, we also have Mass, usually one at 8:30 and another at 10:00 (and one in Spanish at 1:00). The waiting is now over, and we can celebrate the arrival of the Messiah. The readings we hear reflect the story and the joy it brings.

In case you are wondering, though, historically there have been four Masses associated with Christmas: evening vigil, midnight, dawn, and day. In many other places of the world, all four Masses are still celebrated as distinct forms of Christmas Masses.

After Mass, our parishioners go home and enjoy a sumptuous Christmas dinner. Ham, turkey, or tamales form the core of the meal. Which of these is your favorite?

After all that joy, though, I have to add a sobering note. My Boss would want me to remind you that not everyone

Christmas at the Mission

has a family to celebrate Christmas with. Not everyone can afford to give gifts; not everyone receives gifts. Not everyone can afford a special meal (or even a meal at all). So, if you are among the lucky ones who have all that, think about sharing it with those who don't. They are part of God's family, too, and so they are part of your family and my family, our family.

Sula, Parish Cat, San Juan Bautista Mission

Sula, Parish Cat, San Juan Bautista Mission

*O, Christmas tree, O Christmas tree,
how green are your branches...*

Christmas Tree

My favorite story about the Christmas tree, I learned from Fr. Barry Brunsman, who was filling in as a priest when I first came to the Mission. Fr. Barry even wrote a book about the Christmas tree, so you can read about it, too. The book information is listed in the references section at the end of the book you are reading. So, I will tell you a little about Fr. Barry's story of the Christmas tree, and you can read the rest in his book.

The story of the Catholic Christmas tree, according to Fr. Barry, began in the year 724 (approximately). St. Boniface (who wrote a lot about my patron saint, St. Francis) saved a little boy from being sacrificed to two pagan gods, Thor and Odin, said to be "living" inside a giant oak tree. St. Boniface rescued the boy, explained that God wants life, not death, and chopped down the tree. On its stump he placed a little fir tree, sort of like the Christmas trees we use today.

As with many of our Christmas traditions, there is a pagan parallel that began centuries before Jesus was born. Pagans considered evergreen trees to be symbols of life. During the Saturnalia (merrymaking festival dedicated to Saturn), Romans decorated their houses with evergreen branches and hung little dolls from their trees, much like we today decorate our Christmas trees with figurines, as well as lights, cranberry-and-popcorn strings, balls, bells, and other ornaments.

Actually, it was a long time before the Catholic Church selected an official date for Christmas. The Roman Emperor Constantine set December 25th as the date to celebrate Christmas in 336 AD, and a few years later Pope Julius I confirmed that date as Christmas for Catholics. That put Christmas at the same time as the Winter Solstice, so probably some of the customs for celebrating got mixed up and shared. That happens. History can be pretty messy business. Supposedly, the Latvians began using what look like today's Christmas trees in 1510—and the Estonians claimed that they had one in 1441. But, this is surprising, they were one country during part of that time: Livonia.

Well, anyway, all that is a long time ago, so I don't know anyone with first-hand experience to confirm who is right, and there are few written documents. Let's not try to figure this one out; let's just enjoy our Christmas trees!

Did you realize when you were putting up your tree that some of the decorations on the Christmas trees have a special meaning. Think about all the different decorations one can put on a Christmas tree: lights (or in the old days, candles), star, angel, garlands, and tinsel.

Candles, which some people say represent stars, were the first decorations because long ago artificial lights were not possible to make. The light shining from the candle reminded people that Christ is the light of the world. Candles are, of course, dangerous, so over time, in most parts of the world, they have been replaced with artificial lights, which are safer though people in some countries still glue candles, using wax, to Christmas tree branches.

As for the lights that replaced candles, did you know that they used to be very expensive? When they first came out, the Edison Company, which sold them in strands, also rented them because otherwise many people could not afford them. About 20 years later, a teenager named Albert, suggested using colored bulbs, and, developed by NOMA, the Christmas tree lights we know today appeared. Soon thereafter, the lighting of the Christmas tree became a widespread annual secular event. Even the White House has a tree-lighting ceremony, first started by President Calvin Coolidge in 1923.

Christmas at the Mission

A star, representing the Star of Bethlehem often tops a Christmas tree, but there have been other kinds of tops, as well. Way back when, people would put the baby Jesus on top of the tree. Nowadays, angels and stars are the most popular tops.

In addition to using angels as a Christmas tree top, people often hang angels from Christmas tree branches. The angel reminds us of the story of how the angels appeared in the sky above Bethlehem to announce the birth of Jesus. Originally, people made angel ornaments by hand—sometimes as cookies and sometimes crafted from straw. Can you imagine how pretty they must have been! Later, when glassblowers learned how to shape glass into angel figures, glass angels replaced the edible ones. They were better; they lasted longer! But they did not taste as good! Then, the Industrial Revolution made mass-produced angels available, and today we have many different styles of angel ornaments, including some very high-tech varieties that glow, change color, play music, and sing (well, not usually all at the same time, but they can be pretty fancy).

Originally made of flowers and leaves, today garlands (braids) can be made of anything, even popcorn and cranberries. Wound around the green fir branches, they make a Christmas tree look quite festive.

Tinsel is popular for decorating trees. I wonder how many people know the sweet stories behind tinsel? Very early on after decorating fir trees for Christmas gained in popularity, people would sometimes tell their children that angels had decorated the tree. To "prove" that, they would hang tinsel on the tree as hair the angels left behind. There is a competing story that one family was too poor to buy ornaments so, during the night, a kindly spider decorated the tree with webbing (tinsel).!

PS. Don't forget to bless your tree!

Sula, Parish Cat, San Juan Bautista Mission

Sula, Parish Cat, San Juan Bautista Mission

Away in a manger, no crib for a bed...

Creche

The manger where Jesus was born is represented in the church in one of two ways: a creche or a nativity scene. Old Mission has used both, but I like the creche better. I will explain why, but you might be able to guess.

The creche is a little building made out of straw. Inside the creche one sees the scene of the night of Jesus's birth. Mary and Joseph are there. The animals are there. The manger is there, but the manger is empty until Christmas Eve when the priest places the baby Jesus in it. I have to confess that on many occasions during Advent I have fallen asleep in the creche. It is so warm in there, and I feel close to the baby Jesus there. Of course, I scamper out when the priest brings the baby. I know my place—and it is *not* in the manger.

Did you know that my patron saint, St. Francis, created the creche? He did! In 1223, he wanted to create a very special Christmas celebration. You see, St. Francis considered Christmas the most important feast of the year. He wanted to find a way to bring to life—and increase—everyone's admiration of the Christ Child. So, he devised a way to make a realistic representation of the grotto of Bethlehem where Mary gave birth to Jesus, a creche. St. Francis even put live animals in his creche to make it completely realistic. St. Bonaventure quotes St. Francis as saying, "For I wish to do something that will recall to memory the little Child who was born in Bethlehem and set before our bodily eyes in some way the inconvenience of his infant needs." St. Bonaventure relates that St. Francis even obtained the approval of Pope Honorius so he would not get in trouble for inappropriately changing any Christmas traditions. With permission, then, St. Francis set up a creche in the woods near the hermitage in Greccio and filled it with hay saved for the horses. Then, he led an ox and a donkey into the creche. (Wow! That creche was a lot bigger than ours!) When everything was ready, St. Francis was pleased and called the creche "in its glorious simplicity...a symbol of the advent of lowliness, the exaltation of poverty, the praise of humility." Many people came that year and see the creche and, according to Thomas of Celano, a biographer of Francis, "The woods rang with the voices of the crowd and the rocks made answer to their jubilation." Then, they celebrated Mass.

Sometimes churches use nativity scenes instead of creches. Nativity scenes also show Mary, Joseph, animals, and the crib. You can see an example of a nativity scene on the cover of this book. There I am, in the nativity scene, watching over the baby Jesus and being watched over by Mary. What better place to be?

Sula, Parish Cat, San Juan Bautista Mission

*Deck the halls with boughs of holly,
Fa la la la la la, la, la la!...*

Decorations

Christmas decorations fascinate not only Catholics but also everyone living in our community. Informal "competitions" challenge neighbors to try to outdo each other every year in cleverness, beauty, and spectacular design of house and yard decorations.

Lights are everywhere—on trees inside the house and in yards. They come in all kinds of shapes and forms, like icicles or twinkling strings.

Holly, used for decorations, comes from old Druid, Celtic, and Roman traditions as holiday decoration. For Christians, though, the meaning differs: the red berries symbolize the drops of blood that Jesus shed and the prickly leaves symbolize the crown of thorns.

Ivy, typically used together in decorations with holly, has to cling to something in order to grow. For Christians, it symbolizes our need to cling to God in order to grow spiritually.

Have you ever seen a church without poinsettias at Christmas? People bring plant after plant, and they flood our church with red, white, and green color. While there is not clear information about how poinsettias came to be associated with Christmas, some think it has to do with a poor Mexican girl, Pepita. Pepita had no present to bring to the baby Jesus on Christmas Eve. Her cousin, Pedro, cheered her up by telling her that even the smallest gift would make Jesus happy. So, Pepita picked a small bouquet of weeds along the way and put them in the nativity scene. Suddenly, they turned into a beautiful red bouquet, much like poinsettias. These red flowers became famously known as "Flores de Noche Buena" (Flowers of the Holy Night). The red poinsettia leaves symbolize the blood of Christ and the white flowers His purity. (Fun fact: the plant's name comes from Joel Roberts Poinsett, who was the first ambassador to the USA from Mexico and introduced the poinsettia into the USA in 1825; the Latin name of the poinsettia is *Euphorbia pulcherima*, the most beautiful Euphorbia.

Mistletoe is not a Christian tradition, but I will talk about it a little bit because many people confuse this old Norse mythology tradition with modern Christian ones because hanging mistletoe in doorways, hoping to catch someone to kiss, is a very common (secular) thing to do. Sometimes we mistake secular traditions for Christian ones because we have become so used to them existing in parallel with our Catholic traditions. Mistletoe is, ironically, not a very romantic thing at all. It is a parasite! And it is spread through bird poop! Oh, goodness, I hope I have not destroyed anyone's mistletoe-attached romantic inclinations.

Nowadays in our community, Christmas festivities and home decorations appear earlier and earlier. While stores used to hold Christmas sales right after Thanksgiving, some now begin as early as right after Halloween.

Christmas, however, officially begins December 24. One of our previous priests used to repeat over and over, "Christmas decorations go up December 24 (Christmas Eve) and come down January 6 (Epiphany)." After a few years, he stopped repeating that. He said people never listened to him.

Well, that is the way it is with people. Tradition and doctrine may say one thing, but people have a habit of doing another. In this case, perhaps the sheer joy that the Christmas season brings entices them to begin early. Who would not want to have a few more days of Christmas joy? Actually, in some countries, people leave their decorations

Christmas at the Mission

up until Candlemas (the day in early February when Mary and Joseph took Jesus to the Jewish Temple).

Sula, Parish Cat, San Juan Bautista Mission

Sula, Parish Cat, San Juan Bautista Mission

*We three Kings of Orient are bearing gifts;
we traverse afar...*

Epiphany

The Holy Bible contains only 12 mentions of the wise men (magi) and the Star of Bethlehem, but over time they have captured nearly everyone's attention. A Christmas pageant would not be complete without the three magi, or as they are sometimes called, kings. Many nativity scenes also include the three magi. Who were they? What did they see? What did they know? Why are we enthralled with them?

Well, first, they saw a star. The star is called the Star of Bethlehem because when the magi followed it, it stopped in Bethlehem over the manger where Jesus lay.

The magi came from the east, following the star. They seemed to know what the star meant because on the way, they stopped in Jerusalem and asked directions: "Where is the one who has been born King of the Jews? We saw His star in the east and have come to worship him."

Oops! That made King Herod mad and scared. He called the priests together and asked them where the Christ was supposed to be born, and they told him that the prophet Isaiah has written that He would be born in Bethlehem.

After that, King Herod called the magi secretly and asked when they had seen the star. He also asked them to let him know when they found Jesus so he could worship him, too, but he did not really intend to that. Instead, knowing when the magi had seen the star, how far they had come, and how long it should take helped him calculate the age of Jesus at that time.

That was not good, either, because then King Herod could try to find and kill Jesus, which he did try. In fact, he ordered that all babies under the age of two in Bethlehem be killed. Jesus was not among them, though, because his parents had been warned in a dream, and they left Israel before Jesus could be found.

Well, back to the magi. After talking to King Herod, they continued on to Bethlehem, still following the star, which moved ahead of them, showing them the way. Finally, it stopped, and they were able to give their gifts of gold, frankincense, and myrrh to the baby and to worship Him.

When they finished worshipping, they remembered King Herod's words about letting him know the location of Jesus. However, a dream warned them of King Herod's planned treachery, and they went home another way.

Here are some fun facts about the magi.

- Why do we always say three wise men? The Holy Bible does not tell us how many there were. We probably think there were three of them because three gifts were given to Jesus.

- Scholars are not sure where the wise men lived, but they think they came from Iraq, Iran, Saudi Arabia, or Yemen; those places had different names back then: Persia (Iran), Arabia (Iraq and Saudi Arabia), and Sheba (Yemen.) You probably recognize the name, Sheba, because of its famous queen.

- Though they have been *called* kings, there is no evidence that they *were* kings. Actually, the title *magupati* (*magi*) was a title given to priests in the Zoroastrian religion, and they studied the stars like modern astronomers and astrologers; therefore, a star like the Star of Bethlehem which appeared right at the beginning of dawn, which would have been in the East, would have been very significant to them (and it was).

- Given their assumed positions in life—and judging by the gifts they brought—they were probably rich.

This celebration of what the wise men knew and did is called Epiphany. Epiphany means a few things, but all the meanings are connected. It means manifestation (as in a sudden appearance) or it can mean a sudden understanding, realization, or insight. The Epiphany as celebrated in our Catholic customs is God's manifestation of the birth of Jesus to the Gentiles. (Those wise men were not Jewish!)

We have a tradition at our Mission that may have come from Poland or Germany associated with the three kings. We know their names are Caspar, Melchior, and Balthasar. We write C + M + B and the year in roman numerals on a long, narrow piece of paper and put it over our doors to bless our homes for the coming year. These three letters can also stand for *"Christus mansionem benedicat"* ("May Christ Bless This House"). If you visit us at Old Mission San Juan Bautista perhaps you can pick up one of these pieces of paper—or you can make your own.

Sula, Parish Cat, San Juan Bautista Mission

Sula, Parish Cat, San Juan Bautista Mission

A poor orphan girl named Maria was walking to market one day... her offering was lifted to heaven by the very first nightingale's song.

Gifts

One of the main reasons we exchange gifts at Christmas is to remember the gifts that the wise men brought to Jesus. You might say that those three (or more! or fewer!) kings started it all. And today, we get to share in the fun, the awe, the love, and the compassion of gift giving.

St. Nicholas, who became associated with Christmas, was known for bringing gifts. In various countries, on the Feast of St. Nicholas, December 6, people put gifts in shoes, in stockings, and even under pillows. In the United States, we generally put our gifts under the Christmas tree and open them either Christmas Eve or Christmas morning.

We also give gifts throughout the period running up to Christmas. These are gifts to colleagues, friends, at various parties at schools and in other community places. Gift-giving at this time of year is both religious and secular.

At the Mission as at many Catholic churches, we bring gifts for the poor or donate money to buy gifts or food for them for Christmas. Like with other gift-giving, helping those who would not otherwise have a Christmas celebration is as secular an activity as it is a religious one; many organizations contribute to bringing a merry Christmas to everyone.

Finally, think about it. Isn't Christmas a big, huge present that God gave to the world?

Sula, Parish Cat, San Juan Bautista Mission

Sula, Parish Cat, San Juan Bautista Mission

Tell me the story of Jesus; write on my heart every word...

Jesse Tree

In the *Book of Isaiah*, the prophet wrote, "And there shall come forth a rod out of the stem of Jesse, and a Branch shall grow out of his roots." That pretty much is the origin of the Jesse tree.

Jesse was the father of King David, and King David was the bloodline into which Jesus was born. The genealogy of Jesus is read at Mass at Christmas and occasionally at other times. In addition to being called the Son of God and the Son of Man, various Biblical writers refer to him as the Son of David. The Son of David name connects Jesus to the Messiah described by Isaiah and refers to His ability to create miracles and, especially, to heal.

Medieval artists depicted the Jesse tree in various ways, and the first Jesse trees were not ones you could stand on a table. Rather, the pictures were woven into tapestries or formed into glass mosaics. Generally, these pictorial trees showed the lineage of Jesus, the family tree of Jesus.

Today people make charts showing their own family lineage that they call their family trees. They are generally drawn, not physical trees, but they do have branches. So, do you think that perhaps the Jesse tree, which shows Jesus's family, started out family trees of today?

The Jesse tree we have today is generally a small tree with bare branches which we decorate in various ways. (It is a lot like Charlie Brown's Christmas tree, but with a lot more branches.)

Some people use the Jesse tree as an Advent calendar. Each day or each Sunday, they put an ornament on the tree that tells another part of the Christmas story.

Other people hang pieces of paper on the Jesse tree. On each piece of paper is a Holy Bible verse that is special to the person hanging it and generally associated with some aspect of Christmas.

Traditional Jesse trees have a little bit of all of this. So, there are three parts: a tree, ornaments, and Holy Bible verses.

Do you have a Jesse tree at home? If not, for this year (or next), why not try one? Looking up Holy Bible verses and thinking about the Christmas story can only increase a sense of closeness to God, don't you think?

Sula, Parish Cat, San Juan Bautista Mission

Ave Maria, gratia plena...

Mary

Mary, the Mother of Jesus and the mother of the Church, is a very important person to Catholics. At Christmas, we think a lot about Mary. For a very good reason.

When the angel Gabriel came to Mary and announced that God wanted her to bear a child born of spirit, not of flesh, Mary was very young. She could have refused. We all have free will. I mean, I could refuse to do as the Boss asks at the Mission, but goodness, why would I want to do that? Still, I could. If I wanted to.

Someone Mary's age presented with such a proposal must have been scared, but Mary was prepared for this task. She was preserved from sin from the very beginning. That is what Catholics call the Immaculate Conception. We do celebrate the Feast of the Immaculate Conception during Advent, on December 8. This is a Holy Day of Obligation; I suppose everyone knows this.

Some people misunderstand. They confuse the Virgin Birth of Jesus with the Immaculate Conception. They mistakenly think that the Immaculate Conception was Jesus's being conceived of the Holy Spirit. (I can understand how they could be confused. This is not easy stuff to understand. Thank goodness, I am a cat and don't have to understand. I just have to carry out my Mission of helping people.) So, Catholic dogma says that Mary was produced biologically from her mother St. Anne and father Joachim, but God kept her soul free from original sin in order to be ready to bear Jesus. That is the Immaculate Conception: a sinless soul, clean.

The Annunciation, when the angel Gabriel obtained Mary's consent to bear Jesus, is not a feast day during Advent. That comes earlier in the year. I bet everyone thinks about the Annunciation a lot during Advent, though. Without that, there would have been no Christmas—and nothing to wait for.

During Advent we do celebrate another feast associated with Mary on December 12: Our lady of Guadalupe. Our Lady of Guadalupe is very important at our Mission. If you do not know the incredible story, please Google it. In her marvelous appearance in December 1531 in Mexico City to St. Juan Diego, Mary left an unimaginably beautiful image of herself, a likeness of which any visitor can see in many places at the Mission: the church, the chapel, the education center. At the Mission, we celebrate the Feast of Our Lady of Guadalupe with an early Mass followed by breakfast serving *menudo* and *pan dulce*.

I could say a lot more about Mary. Many people have written many books about her. Of course, Catholics already know a lot about her. My little book is too small to hold the grandness of Mary, so I will just stop and say simply that I love to sit or sleep at the feet of Mary (as you can see from the front and back covers of this book). If you have not done so, you should try it sometime!

Sula, Parish Cat, San Juan Bautista Mission

*Gentle woman, quiet light,
morning star, so strong and bright...*

Mary Candle

What better represents Christmas than white candles" Big white candles? They exude beauty and warmth; they each have a meaning.

The Mary candle and the Christ candle look very much alike—because the Christ candle is the basic part of the Mary candle. The Mary candle adds a few adornments. First, there is a blue ribbon wrapped around the candle. Second, often, there is a white silk cloth that the blue ribbon ties together onto the candle.

The Mary candle is placed before an image of Our Lady—an icon or a statue. Catholics make entreaties of Mary—or just talk to her. Some families decorate a Christ candle as a Mary candle on the Feast of the Immaculate Conception. Other families set out their Mary candle for all of the Advent season.

Regularly, throughout the Advent season, the candle is lit for dinner. The candle reminds each family member to keep his or her own light of grace burning, like Mary did, in order to be prepared for the arrival of the Messiah.

What a beautiful scene! Taking it apart makes it even more beautiful. Each part holds special significance:

- The candle holder represents the rod bearing a flower (Mary), coming from the root of Jesse, from which Jesus will be born.

- The white candle itself, the Christ candle, represents Christ, the Light of the World, who will take away all darkness.

- The white silk cloth tells of the purity and simplicity of Mary, i.e. the Mother of Jesus.

- The blue ribbon, the color of the dress which Mary is typically shown wearing, holds everything together.

You can make a Mary candle very easily. Just start with the Christ candle, which you can buy in many places. You can also buy Mary candles. Some Mary candles today have pictures on them, such as Our Lady of Guadalupe. I like the simple white ones, but being a cat, I am not allowed around candles unless others are near me.

For more information about candles, if you skipped the earlier section, please go back and read it. I tried to stuff it full of lots of information for you!

Sula, Parish Cat, San Juan Bautista Mission

Our Father, who are in Heaven...

Prayer

There are many different prayers for Christmas. You probably already know dozens. If not, well, there's any Catholic gift shop! Since I cannot list all the different, beautiful prayers that people recite at Christmas, I will tell you about two special kinds that Old Mission San Juan Bautista parishioners pray a lot: novenas and rosary prayers.

A novena is a 9-day prayer. At Christmas special novenas are prayed. St. Andrew's novena begins November 30, the feast day of St. Andrew, the first apostle called by Jesus. St. Andrew's novena is more than 100 years old. Here are the beautiful words:

> *Hail and blessed be the hour and moment in which the Son of God of the most pure Virgin Mary, at midnight, in Bethlehem in the piercing cold. In that hour vouchsafe, I beseech Thee, O my God, to hear my prayer and grant my desires through the merits of Our Savior Jesus Christ and of His Blessed Mother. Amen.*

The Rosary, as you can see in the picture, is a string of 50 prayer beads in groups of ten, called a decade, given to Saint Dominic by Our Lady in an apparition in 1214. The word, *rosary*, means *garland of roses*. There are four kinds of mysteries that can be prayed on the Rosary. During Christmas parishioners pray the Joyful Mysteries.

Christmas rosaries can be made from beads of Christmas colors. The words that are spoken on each of the beads is standard:

- On the crucifix, make the sign of the cross and then pray the Apostles' Creed.

- On the next large bead, say the Our Father.

- On the following three small beads, pray three Hail Marys.

- On the chain, pray the Glory Be.

- On the large bead, meditate on the first mystery and pray the Our Father.

- On each decade, start with the Lord's Prayer, followed by 10 Hail Marys, followed by a Glory Be, and finish with the prayer for the next joyful mystery, which is the entrance into the following decade.

The Chaplet of the Divine Mercy is prayed on the Rosary, with the prayers on the Our Father bead differing from the usual words and referring to mercy. Then there is an optional closing prayer for mercy:

O Blood and Water, which gushed forth from the Heart of Jesus as a fountain of Mercy for us, I trust in You! Eternal God, in whom mercy is endless and the treasury of compassion inexhaustible, look kindly upon us and increase Your mercy in us, that in difficult moments we might not despair nor become despondent, but with great confidence submit ourselves to

I am not telling you anything that you probably don't know. If this is news to you, then think about finding instructions for the Rosary and the Chaplet of Mercy on line or at any Catholic gift shop.

    I know these things are taught in catechism classes because sometimes I end up eavesdropping on them. I suppose, though, if you do not pray the Rosary regularly, it is quite possible to forget how to do it. Thank goodness, there are always catechists around to help, gift shops to sell, the Internet to instruct, and cats like me to remind you.

Sula, Parish Cat, San Juan Bautista Mission

Sula, Parish Cat, San Juan Bautista Mission

The first noel the angel did say was to certain poor shepherds in fields where they lay...

Shepherds

Who can imagine a Christmas pageant without shepherds? They played such an important role on Christmas Eve!

So, as the story is told by Luke, shepherds were out in the fields on Christmas Eve, minding their own business, taking care of their sheep, and probably dozing off at times. Then, suddenly an angel appeared to them from high in the sky. The light of God that surrounded the angel terrified the shepherds, but the angel said to them, "Do not be afraid."

Then, the angel told the shepherds the story of the Messiah and how he had just been born in the town of Bethlehem (also known, appropriately, as the town of David). The angel told the shepherds that they would find the Messiah as a baby, swaddled, and lying in a manger.

Well, if that was not enough to disturb their quiet night on the hillside, imagine their shock when suddenly a large choir of angels appeared in the heavens, singing and praising God:

"Glory to God in the highest heaven, and on earth peace to those on whom his favor rests."

Of course, as soon as the angels disappeared, the shepherds hurried off to Bethlehem. Wouldn't you after all that?

The shepherds found Mary, Joseph, and Jesus. Then they ran out and spread the good news to anyone who would listen.

Isn't it interesting that the angels did not visit the religious leaders, the kind, or rich people? Instead, God sent the angels to humble shepherds, who, of course, being the raisers of Passover lambs, would know what sacrifice meant and would understand the significance of the Messiah. That tells us something about what God values, doesn't it?

Sula, Parish Cat, San Juan Bautista Mission

Chestnuts roasting on an open fire...

St. Lucy Cakes

St. Lucy, who grew up to be a virgin and martyr, lost her father at the age of 5. Raising a daughter as a single parent and no protector, Lucy's mother wanted to marry her early so that she knew she was taken care of. Lucy, however, had other ideas. She had dedicated her virginity to God and wanted to give her dowry to the poor. As the story goes, she told her mother, "What you give away right before you die does not count for much because you cannot take it with you. Give now to the true Savior what you would have saved to your death."

Unfortunately, Lucy's suitor was not pleased with this idea, and as she began distributing her wealth to the poor, her suitor denounced her to the governor of Syracuse (in Sicily, Italy), where they lived. The governor agreed that she was behaving poorly and ordered her to burn a sacrifice to the image of the emperor. When Lucy refused to worship the emperor, the governor order her to be sent to a brothel, but when the guards came to take her away, they could not move her. So, they heaped kindling around her and tried to set her on fire, but the wood would not burn. Finally, they ran her through with a sword, and she died. She was 21. The year was 304. The emperor was Diocletian. And many Christians were persecuted and martyred while he ruled.

Some unconfirmed reports say that Lucy was tortured before being killed, and her eyes were gouged out. That might explain why she is considered the patron saint of the blind.

The feast of St. Lucy is on December 13th. A couple of traditions are associated with the Feast of St. Lucy."

One tradition is to walk or drive around neighborhoods and look at the lights. Light-viewing is quite appropriate since St. Lucy's name means "light." In fact, there is a legend that says Lucy wore a crown on her head that had candles on it to light the way to the poor when she was bringing them food.

The other tradition has to do with Christmas baking, in this case, St. Lucy cakes. The traditional St. Lucy cakes are saffron buns. They can also be made pretty easily from canned cinnamon rolls (I vote for easy, though I suppose, for people, the taste would be different. For me, well, I am a cat. I don't eat St. Lucy cakes or any cakes or buns or rolls, for that matter.)

Here is a list of other foods associated with Christmas.

- Eggnog
- Fruitcake
- Nuts, including roasted chestnuts
- Candy canes (Hmm, is candy food?)
- Christmas cookies
- Gingerbread
- Tamales
- Ponche Navideño Mexicano
- Pozole
- Menudo

Can you think of others?

No one has to be restricted to foods that are especially associated with Christmas. Lots of people like to spend a little extra time baking during the Christmas holidays. They show their love of family and friends (and even strangers) by making things for them, things that look pretty and taste good—to people.

Well, for all my human friends: *bon appetit!*

Sula, Parish Cat, San Juan Bautista Mission

Sula, Parish Cat, San Juan Bautista Mission

Jolly old Saint Nicholas, lean your ear this way...

St. Nicholas

December 6 is the feast day of Saint Nicholas; it is also probably the day on which he died—no one knows for sure which date he died. Often considered the same as Santa Claus in the secular community, St. Nicholas was a real person—and not the St. Nick or Santa Claus dominating Christmas activities in the secular community although he may have served as the model for them.

Saint Nicholas was born in Turkey, around the year 280. Although he became an orphan as a young man, his parents left him a good inheritance. Nicholas used this inheritance to help the sick and poor.

Later, Nicholas became the bishop of Myra. As bishop, he wore many colors of robes. Red was his favorite. So, it is not surprising that the characters developed in his image, such as Santa Claus, also dress in red.

St. Nicholas did many kindnesses and often brought people gifts. One legend says that he saved three daughters of one father who did not have enough money to pay their dowries. St. Nicholas came to the father's house three times, each time putting a bag of money inside, enough to pay for one dowry. In another instance of kindness, he saved three men from prison. Very often, he secretly gave gifts to people who needed them.

St. Nicholas, like St. Lucy, ran up against Emperor Diocletian. The emperor exiled St. Nicholas from Myra and later put him prison.

After St. Nicholas died, many miracles became associated with him. For this reason, people started calling him

Sula, Parish Cat, San Juan Bautista Mission

St. Nicholas the Wonder Worker. He became known as a guardian of children, protector of children, and liberal gift-giver.

Many other legends about St. Nicholas exist, but there are too few documents to confirm most of these stories. One story, unconfirmed, tells of sailors in trouble on a choppy sea off the coast of Turkey. They asked the now-dead St. Nicholas to help them, and he appeared on their deck. He calmed them and the sea, and they were able to sail their ship to port. Now, on December 6, the sailors in Bari (Italy) carry the statue of St. Nicholas from the Cathedral there that is named after him and that contains his relics out to sea so that St. Nicholas can bless the water and give them safe passage all year long.

In some parts of the world, new traditions sprang up associated with St. Nicholas. In Holland, for example, the children would put out their shoes at night and discover in the morning what St. Nicholas had left them. Some say that the Christmas stockings hung up by American children to be filled by Santa Claus are an example of St. Nicholas being adopted in the American secular culture. In Czechoslovakia, one day during Advent, parents gather their children together. The children sit on chairs while three figures stand in front of them: an angel on the left, St. Nicholas in the middle, and the devil on the right. For each child, St. Nicholas reads a list of the child's actions during the year, both good and bad, and then determines whether there were more good or bad ones. If there are more good ones, the angel can give the child a gift. If there are more bad ones, then the devil is allowed to carry the child off in a bag. Those kids are scared!! Their parents say that they behave very well for at least 3-4 months after that! I can imagine. I think I would, too. If it were really St. Nicholas, though, I think he would just reach out a hand and help the child who had been naughty because, after all, St. Nicholas is best known for his kindness.

Sula, Parish Cat, San Juan Bautista Mission

Sula, Parish Cat, San Juan Bautista Mission

The ivy and the holly are both full well grown...

Wreaths

Wreaths are usually associated with Advent. People tell me that the Germans were the first to make wreaths. Some say that the wreath is the most common custom associated with Advent, but I don't know about that. After all, those Advent calendars are very popular, too.

Wreaths are made in a circle. The circle symbolizes eternity and Jesus's immortality. Also, a wreath is usually made from evergreen branches, another symbol of eternity.

The word *wreath* means to *twist*. The easiest way to make a wreath is to use a wire and bend it into a circle. Then you can bind green evergreen branches to the wire. So, the wreath is an evergreen circle. As such, it reminds us that there were many years from the creation of the world and the days of Adam and Eve to the birth of Jesus. After all, the green of the evergreen trees, like firs, lasts year in and year out, a long time, just like the long time it took to get from Adam to the appearance of that very special baby.

If a wreath is made of holly, it carries the meaning of the holly. The red berries represent the blood of Jesus, and the sharp, pointy leaves represent the crown of thorns.

You know how many other years have passed, like an evergreen tree that goes on and on? More than two thousand—since the birth and death of Jesus and our waiting for His second coming. Staying ever green in our hope and faith.

One special wreath that I talked about earlier is the Advent wreath, which has four candles. Of course, there are many other kinds of wreaths without candles. Wreaths are used to decorate churches, homes, business, work places, and all sorts of locations. There are even electronic wreaths beamed onto the sides of houses.

Some people hold Advent wreath ceremonies. You can find many prayers and hymns online that you can use if you want to hold an Advent wreath ceremony.

Christians have not been the only users of wreaths. The Romans hung wreaths on their doors as declarations of victory. Rich women in Rome wore wreaths on their heads as dress-up for special occasions.

Merry Christmas

from

Santa Claus (USA)
Père Noël (France)
Ded Moroz (Russia)

And all the other secular enactments
of the wonderful St. Nicholas!

And from me:
*Meows and prayers for a blessed new year
filled with peace and joy!*

Sula, Parish Cat, San Juan Bautista Mission

References and Sources for More Information

Apostleship of Prayer. 2017. *Sacred Reading for Advent and Christmas 2017-2018*. Ave Maria Press. [A little meow: Although this book is meant for the year in which I am writing this book, the readings can be for any year.]

Bauer, Judy. 2001. Advent and Christmas with Fulton J. Sheen: *Daily Scripture and Prayers Together with Sheen's Own Words*. Liguori Publications. [A little meow: Prayers never grow old.]

Brunsman, Barry, O.F.M. 2006. *The Christmas Tree: Its Origin and Meaning*. San Juan Bautista, CA: St. Francis Ministries.

Suffin, Rev. Edward J. 1955. *True Christmas Spirit*. St. Meinrad, Indiana: Grail Publications.

Carroll, Kathleen M. and Sr. Rose Pacatte. 2001. *A Catholic Christmas*. St. Anthony Messenger Press.

Cleary, John. 2015. *Advent and Christmas Wisdom from Pope Francis*. Liguori Publications.

Kelly, Joseph F. 2004. *The Origins of Christmas*. Liturgical Press.

Noel, Marie. 2012. *Catholic Christmas Prayers*. BooksByNoel.

Rega. Frank M. 2007. *St. Francis of Assisi and the Conversion of the Muslims*. TAN Books and Publishers.

Saunders, Rev. William "St. Francis and the Christmas Creche." *Arlington Catholic Herald*.

Saward, John. 2002. *Cradle of Redeeming Love: The Theology of the Christmas Mystery*. Ignatius Press.

Thomas of Celano. 2004. *The Francis Trilogy: The Life of St. Francis*. New City Press.

Wensell, Paloma and Ulises Wensell. 2012. *The Christmas Star*. Liturgical Press.

Zimmerman, Mike and Sarah Zimmerman. 2017. *Little Catholic Clubhouse and the True Meaning of Christmas*. Little Catholic Clubhouse Publishing.

If you liked this book and want to see lots more pictures, think about buying or borrowing my other books.

Surviving Cancer, Healing People: One Cat's Story is available at bookstores, on line, and at Old Mission San Juan Bautista Gift Shop and St. Francis Retreat Center in San Juan Bautista.

Tale of a Mission Cat, my second book, is also available at the same places as my first book.

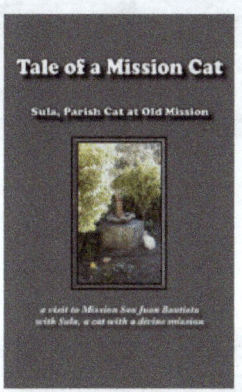

If your library does not have my books, please ask the acquisitions librarian to get a copy not just for you but for any cat lovers and Mission lovers in your community and maybe, as well, those who want to spend some time reflecting on their faith.

Also, watch for my next book. I am writing it right now. It is called *Saints I know*. It is also to be published by MSI Press and should be available on June 24, 2018, the feast day of St. Francis, my patron saint. I hope that it will be interesting to anyone who wants to become familiar with more saints, especially to children in catechism classes (and maybe helpful to the catechists as well).

You can read more stories about me and see more pictures here:

California newspapers:

"Mission Cat's Story Is a Tale of Hope." Benitolink (Laureen Diephof). November 1, 2016. https://benitolink.com/mission-cats-story-tale-hope

"A Cat's Mission." *Hollister Freelance* (Katie Helland, author; Nick Lovejoy/Studio Lovejoy, photographer). January 7 2016, pages B1, B15-16. http://www.sanbenitocountytoday.com/lifestyles/sula-the-cat-is-on-a-mission-in-san-juan/article_813c16f6-b575-11e5-886b-cfab711d8975.html

"Sula the Cat Is on a Mission in San Juan." *Morgan Hill Times* (Katie Helland). January 7, 2016. http://www.morganhilltimes.com/sula-the-cat/image_2a14d475-2f16-548a-a08d-62aa914fcd23.html (Yes, it is the same story—for different readers.)

Guideposts Magazine:

Photo from Guideposts Magazine by Martin Klimek Photography

"Cat with a Mission." (Elizabeth Mahlou). *Guideposts Magazine.* December 2015. Pages 60-63.

"Family Room." *Guideposts Magazine.* December 2015, Pages 79-80.

"Sula, a Cat with a Divine Mission." https://www.guideposts.org/slideshow/sula-a-cat-with-a-divine-mission

Blog Interview

My interview with Mudpie, the Cat: http://www.mochasmysteriesmeows.com/2016/09/mudpie-interviews-sula-old-mission-san.html

Most important, follow my adventures on my Face Book page, Sula, by friending me. Or, just like me! https://www.facebook.com/Sula-909598572467537/. More pictures! More stories! And I will answer you!

Proceeds from this book will be used to help restore, retrofit, and preserve Old Mission San Juan Bautista.

Tax-deductible contributions may be made online to the fund at www.oldmissionsjb.org. Or, a check made out to "Save Mission San Juan Bautista" may be mailed to

Old Mission San Juan Bautista
P. O. Box 400
San Juan Bautista, CA 95045

Please note, if you don't mind, that this is a donation in the name of Sula—unless, of course, you prefer to donate in the name of someone special to you. All donations are welcome!

Thank you for helping to save my home!
Sula

www.ingramcontent.com/pod-product-compliance
Lightning Source LLC
LaVergne TN
LVHW050625090426
835512LV00007B/667